THE
BROTHERS
AND THEIR
LUNCH BASKET

NICOLE BRAN CLARK

THE BROTHERS AND THEIR LUNCH BASKET

© 2026 by Nicole Bran Clark

All rights reserved. Published 2026

DO NOT REPRODUCE WITHOUT PERMISSION

Some design elements of this book were produced with the assistance of artificial intelligence tools.

Published in the United States of America by

www.spiritmedia.us

Spirit Media and our logos are trademark of
Spirit Media Inc
205 S Academy Street St #3251
Cary, NC 27519
1 (888) 800-3744

Juvenile Fiction | Religious | Christian | Early Readers

Paperback ISBN: 979-8-89307-186-3
eBook ISBN: 979-8-89307-173-3
PDF ISBN: 979-8-89307-174-0
Library of Congress Control Number: 2026902881

Note from the Author

This story, The Brothers and Their Lunch Basket, is a creative re-telling of the miracle of Jesus feeding the 5,000. While the miracle is drawn from the Bible, the characters and some events are fictional, designed to help young readers engage with the story in a fun and imaginative way.

We encourage readers to remember that the Bible tells the true account, and this story adds creative elements to help children understand and enjoy the message more deeply.

The morning sun peeked through the window as the smell of pancakes filled the kitchen. Ima was already up, cooking breakfast like she always did.

Asher was the first to bounce in, eyes wide with curiosity. "Ima, why does the sky turn orange before the sun comes up?" he asked.

Elijah burst in right behind him, still tying his shoes, ready for whatever adventure the day might bring. Samuel followed slowly, his brow furrowed as he checked the weather through the window—always the careful one. And last came David, quietly humming a tune, gently pulling out chairs for his brothers. He liked when everyone got along.

It was a normal morning for the four brothers—as normal as mornings could be in their little home.

After breakfast, they pushed their chairs back, grabbed their satchels, and made their way to the door.

"Thank you for breakfast, Ima. Love you!" they called out in unison, planting quick kisses on her cheek.

"Wait! Don't forget your lunch!" Ima said, holding up a woven basket

Asher skidded to a stop, ran back, and grabbed the basket filled with their food.

On their way to school, Elijah noticed a big commotion. "What's going on?" Elijah asked.

"I don't know, but I don't want to be late for school," Samuel replied.

"Oh, who cares if we're late! Let's go look!" Elijah said, running toward the crowd.

The other brothers looked at each other, shrugged, and followed him.

They saw a HUGE crowd—too many people to count! Men, women, and children were talking, laughing, and playing.

Some sat in the grass, others stood in circles, and even babies were there!

As they took in the lively scene, David's attention was drawn to a smaller group of men standing aside, their faces marked with concern.

14

"Hey, let's go see what they are talking about," David whispered to Asher.

The brothers quietly approached, hiding behind a tree to listen in.

15

"Philip, where are we to buy bread so these people can eat?" a man asked.

He had olive skin, big brown eyes, and brown hair.

Philip's eyes widened. "I don't know! There are too many people. We don't have enough money for that!"

Asher looked at their lunch basket. "David, what if we gave them our lunch?"

"I know it's not much—just five loaves of bread and two fish—but I can't stop thinking about all those hungry faces. Maybe it could help."

"Are you crazy?! Then we will be hungry and without any food for our lunch."

"But David, remember how Ima always says that when we share what we have, even if it's just a little, God can use it to bless many?"

"She says that's how we show His love."

"You're right Asher, they do need our help. We'll be okay."

Before David could finish saying we'll be okay, Asher walked toward the group. The man with brown eyes looked at Asher and smiled gently.

"Um, hello, sir. I'm sorry to bother you, but my brothers and I heard you need food. It's not much, but... you can have our lunch."

Philip took the basket and glanced at the man beside him. The man nodded with a warm smile.

"Thank you for sharing," Philip said.

The man on the other side who they called Jesus looked at Asher with a warm smile.

Asher turned and ran back to his brothers.

21

"Asher did WHAT?!" Elijah shouted, eyes wide.

"I'm going to be hungry," Samuel groaned.

David shrugged. "You'll be okay. Ima always says we're blessed to be a blessing."

David started walking toward the school.

"Wait! Don't you want to see what happens?" Asher asked, still breathless from the excitement.

"Why?" David replied. "There's not enough food for everyone."

Asher stood his ground. "I don't care. I want to watch."

The man they called Jesus asked the crowd to sit in smaller groups.

He took the basket, lifted it up, prayed, and gave thanks to God.

Then, they began passing out the bread and fish.

"What is he doing?" Elijah asked, eyes wide with disbelief.

"There isn't even enough for one small group!"

Yet, as they watched, something incredible unfolded before them.

The basket seemed to have no end—more bread, more fish!

It was as if the food multiplied with every reach, filling everyone with wonder.

The brothers watched in awe, their eyes widening with each passing moment, as the seemingly endless supply of food from their basket fed thousands.

Suddenly, David gasped. "Guys! We're so late for school!"

At school, none of the brothers could concentrate; they couldn't stop thinking about what they had seen.

Asher stared at his lunch cubby, wondering if it still held a miracle.

Elijah fiddled with his pencil during read-aloud time, eyes far away.

Samuel raised his hand to answer a math question then forgot what he was going to say.

David doodled loaves and fish all over his worksheet.

They passed each other in the hallway. But none of them had the chance to say what they were really thinking.

That had to wait until after school. As soon as the final school bell rang, they rushed to find each other.

On the way home, they talked excitedly.

"Did you see how every time they reached in, more food came out?! How is that possible?" Asher asked.

None of them knew the answer.

When they arrived home Ima kissed each of them on the head and smiled.

But before they could say a word, Ima gently asked, "Did you boys remember to be kind today?"

"We shared our lunch," David blurted out.

"And somehow... it fed everyone!"

Ima knelt down and looked at them, her eyes soft.

The boys looked at each other, amazed all over again. "You see, when we offer what little we have with love, God can turn it into more than we ever imagined. That's why we always share—because you never know what miracle He might do with it."

The boys looked at each other, amazed all over again.

"I guess you were right, Ima," Elijah said.

"Sharing really is powerful."

Note to Parents, Teachers, and Ministry Leaders

The Brothers & Their Lunch Basket was written to help children imagine themselves as part of one of Jesus' most famous miracles—the feeding of the five thousand. Through the eyes of four brothers with unique personalities, children can explore important values like generosity, obedience, curiosity, and faith.

This story offers a springboard for deeper conversations about how God can use even small offerings in big ways when we choose to share and trust Him.

How to Use This Book:

- **Read-aloud with expression** to help young listeners engage emotionally and visually with the story.

- **Pause to ask questions like:**
    "What would you have done if you were Asher?"
    "Have you ever shared something and watched God bless it?"
    "Which brother do you relate to most and why?"

- **Discuss biblical truth** by reading John 6:1-14 together. Talk about how Jesus multiplied the loaves and fish, and what that teaches us about faith and compassion.

- **Use the brothers' personalities** as a way to affirm your child's God-given traits:

>Curiosity is a gift.

>Adventurous hearts can lead others.

>Cautious thinkers help keep everyone grounded.

>Peacemakers reflect the heart of Jesus.

Whether you're a parent, teacher, family member, Sunday school teacher, or small group leader, this story is a tool for nurturing both faith and imagination. Let it inspire children to believe that God can use them—just as they are—to make a difference in the world.